Original title:
The Green Line

Copyright © 2025 Creative Arts Management OÜ
All rights reserved.

Author: Aurora Sinclair
ISBN HARDBACK: 978-1-80567-032-2
ISBN PAPERBACK: 978-1-80567-112-1

The Balance of Greenery and Grit

In a city where plants wear shoes,
And trees gossip over local news,
The flowers argue who's the best-dressed,
While weeds claim they simply need a rest.

Squirrels in ties debate the rate,
Of acorn stocks—it's quite a fate!
Rabbits throw parties with veggies galore,
While bugs break-dance on the forest floor.

Birds don hats, the peacocks strut,
While the slugs just slide in a muddy rut,
Everyone's laughing, even the stones,
As nature juggles both laughs and groans.

So here's to the chaos, the beauty, the mess,
Where greenery thrives, and critters impress,
With a wink and a nod, let's finally see,
Life's a wild show, and we're all VIP!

Promenade of Leaves

On strolls where whispers sway,
A leaf slipped right, got lost in play.
Another spun, a cheeky tease,
They giggled soft in the gentle breeze.

A squirrel danced in comic flair,
Wore an acorn like a hat, quite rare.
He jumped and jived, oh what a scene,
While branches shrugged, 'What could it mean?'

Junction of Dreams

At crosswalks where the shadows merge,
A butterfly chose to take the verge.
With fluttering wings, it led the way,
While ants declared, 'We too shall play!'

A frog in a helmet croaked with glee,
'I'm off to conquer this world, you see!'
But every leap was just a spree,
As cars went by, he filmed his plea.

Tapestry of Growth

In gardens bright where gnomes may grumble,
 The daisies played in their own humble.
 They waved their heads, a flower dance,
While bees all buzzed, they took a chance.

A snail in rainboots joined the fray,
'What a fine day! Let's glide and sway!'
 But who was fastest in this race?
The grass laughed loud—oh, what a chase!

Lush Echoes

In a forest thick, the echoes burst,
Where laughter was an earthy thrust.
The mushrooms giggled, hid in a nook,
Told stories wild in their woodland book.

A cat with flair sang to the trees,
With a tune that danced upon the breeze.
The branches swayed, they clapped in delight,
As laughter filled the soft, warm night.

Flora's Embrace

In a garden where ferns do dance,
A gnome tries to wear a flower's pants.
Buzzing bees in a silly race,
They bump and sway in this leafy place.

A dandelion wears a crown of fluff,
It puffs out seeds saying, "That's enough!"
Laughing buds in riotous cheer,
Declare that spring has brought good beer.

Trails of Tranquility

A squirrel with shades on struts around,
While pondering why nuts can't be found.
Chasing shadows, he strikes a pose,
On a trail where no one knows.

A rabbit with sneakers hops and skips,
While avoiding the ants and their little trips.
With every bounce, he starts to sing,
About the joy that nature can bring.

Connection Through Green

Two trees whisper secrets of the breeze,
One tells the other about his knees.
With twisted roots and branches wide,
They chuckle at squirrels who always hide.

A patch of grass plays peek-a-boo,
While mushrooms gossip with morning dew.
Nature's sitcom, each scene a thrill,
As petals giggle on the windowsill.

Verdure's Song

A vine sings softly to a fence,
"Stop growing out, it's sheer nonsense!"
With twirls and curls, it locks in cheer,
While the fence replies, "You're the best, my dear!"

Frogs in hats croak songs so bold,
Sharing secrets in the ferny fold.
In this patch of joy, laughter prevails,
As the wind whispers funny tales.

Stories Woven in Wild Greens

In a forest thick with tales,
The squirrels plot their grand fails,
Leaves rustle with gossip and glee,
As bunnies hop off with their tea.

Moss blankets like a soft bed,
While deer dance dreams in their head,
The chipmunks compete in a race,
Tripping over their own tiny space.

The whispers of branches like jokes,
Tickling the ribs of the folks,
Who stumble upon a toadstool feast,
Where laughter is never the least.

So take a stroll through this glee,
Where every leaf holds a guarantee,
That nature's humor is rich and bold,
In the stories of greens, joy unfolds.

Following the Curl of the Fern

The ferns twist their fronds in delight,
As we stumble through day and night,
Our shoes covered in dirt and grass,
Hoping none of it will last!

With every curl, a giggle spills,
Tickling the air with playful thrills,
A squirrel drops acorns with flair,
Causing all of us to stop and stare.

Rabbits hop with mischief in mind,
In shadows, wonders are entwined,
Chasing bugs that dance in the sun,
Leaving behind chaos and fun.

So let's follow where the ferns lead,
Finding joy in nature's creed,
For every twist brings a chuckle near,
In the curls of greens, there's nothing to fear.

Along the Borders of Breath

Where whispers of green start to play,
We find ourselves lost in the fray,
Breath held tight, laughter bursts free,
As raccoons steal snacks with great glee.

The breeze carries secrets untold,
With every rustle, the humor unfolds,
A hedgehog grins beneath a tree,
Poking fun at all who run free.

Caterpillars waltz with great pride,
Thinking they're stars in this leafy ride,
But with one shake, they tumble down,
Chuckling softly, they don't wear a frown.

So stroll along this cheery edge,
Where laughter and greens make a pledge,
To tickle your heart with every breath,
In nature's spread, we dance 'til death.

A Corridor of Nature's Embrace

Welcome to a hallway of green,
Where every corner reveals a scene,
Bumblebees buzzing with a tune,
As flowers giggle 'neath the moon.

Leaves shake hands in joking delight,
While owls hoot "Who's winning the fight?"
The raccoons peer with a crafty grin,
Plotting mischief just to begin.

Sunbeams giggle, tickling the ground,
As shadows of laughter twirl all around,
A playful snail in a slow-motion chase,
Squeezing in joy, what a pretty face!

So take a step in this fun-filled space,
Let nature's humor set the pace,
For in this corridor of delight,
Every nook holds funny sights.

Nature's Radiance

In the garden, gnomes all dance,
Wearing hats like they own the chance.
Flowers giggle, trees wear grins,
Nature's humor truly spins.

Bumblebees buzz with a joke to share,
Pollen parties fill the air.
Ladybugs play hide and seek,
Their laughter echoes with each squeak.

Worms debate the best route to take,
While frogs hop, making ripples awake.
Sunshine winks through leafy threads,
Tickling the noses of sleepy heads.

When raindrops laugh and puddles pop,
Every raindancer gives their hop.
Nature's radiance never fades,
In this joyful green parade!

Flow of Inspiration

Streams of thought wiggle and flow,
Silly fish wear hats, steal the show.
Frogs with briefcases leap and glide,
In this world, nonsense is our guide.

Ducks in shades cross the busy stream,
Planning a party, living the dream.
Leaves sing songs of adventure anew,
Creating laughter, prompting 'who knew?'

Squirrels with acorns become the jest,
Competing for the funniest dressed.
Inspiration flows in every trend,
As nature giggles with a playful bend.

When flowers write their quirky verse,
Even the thorns start to converse.
In the heart of the wild, we find cheer,
Flowing joy, so crystal clear!

Ecology's Embrace

Trees give hugs to the birds so bright,
Chasing grasshoppers into the night.
Rabbits toss bunnies in a race,
While squirrels sneak snacks, just in case.

The moose wears a crown made of leaves,
Claiming the forest, everyone's pleased.
Insects parade in funky attire,
While crickets play tunes around the fire.

Wildflowers compete for the best dress,
Each petal's a story, never a mess.
In the embrace of this eco-lot,
Laughter is found in the wisdom it taught.

Time slips away with a giggle and jest,
In nature's arms, we feel so blessed.
Embracing the quirk, we join as one,
Ecology's humor shines just like the sun!

Harmony's Veil

Dancing shadows on the green floor,
Whispering secrets, always wanting more.
Harmony giggles with a light breeze,
While branches clink like parties at ease.

Songs of the owl make everyone laugh,
As the brook plans its comedic path.
Leaves rustle softly, they share a joke,
As laughter rises like soft smoke.

Clouds are doodles in the big blue sky,
Bringing spectacles, by and by.
Together we roll in nature's bliss,
Each moment of joy, we dare not miss.

Harmony's veil wraps us tight,
In this rhyming world, everything's right.
With smiles abundant, we join the band,
Swaying in rhythms of this green land!

Abode of Blossoms

In a garden patch, I found a gnome,
Wearing a hat, he looked like a dome.
He tried to dance but tripped on a bean,
Spinning 'round, he couldn't be seen.

Birds chirped loudly, laughing away,
A squirrel joined in for a grand ballet.
They twirled and whirled with great delight,
While I just watched, giggling at sight.

A pink flamingo took a selfie too,
Posing with daisies, oh what a view!
The flowers waved as if to say,
'This gnome's a star, it's his lucky day!'

With laughter and blooms, the time flew fast,
In this quirky realm, worries can't last.
Instead of frowns, we blossomed in cheer,
In this wacky abode, joy's ever near.

Nature's Embrace

In a world where trees like giants grow,
A bear in sunglasses gives quite a show.
He taught the birds how to salsa dance,
While rabbits hopped off in a wild prance.

A turtle played tunes on a leafy flute,
Making the flowers jiggle and hoot.
The river giggled, doing its thing,
Flowing in rhythm with the songs they sing.

A raccoon wore a tiny bright hat,
Juggling acorns, and oh, what of that!
The stars above began to twinkle bright,
As nightfall came, they joined in delight.

Nature's a stage, with humor galore,
Surprises await behind every door.
So take a seat, let your worries erase,
In this comical, wild embrace.

Canvassed Journeys

We painted the sky with shades of blue,
A chicken joined in, hand-in-hand, too.
With a brush in beak and a flair for art,
It dashed around, acting quite smart.

The sun wore shades, looking quite chill,
While clouds shaped bunnies, oh what a thrill!
As colors blended, a rainbow burst,
A unicorn passed by, quenching its thirst.

Marshmallow bushes grew tall and wide,
And jellybean rivers flowed with pride.
The laughter echoed through canny trees,
As silly creatures danced with the breeze.

Adventures await on this whimsical road,
Where humor and colors are freely bestowed.
Pack up your giggles, let the fun start,
In this canvassed journey, there's room for art!

A Journey Realized

On a toadstool train, we took to the rail,
With mice as conductors, we set off to sail.
The engine coughed up clouds of bright smoke,
As everyone laughed, with not a word spoke.

Kangaroos bounced by, wearing top hats,
While penguins read books, addressing the chats.
Twirling in circles, we lost track of time,
As giggles erupted like a well-tuned rhyme.

Moments flitted past like butterflies bright,
Juggling and leaping, oh what a sight!
As the train pulled in, we cheered and we grinned,
A journey well spent, with laughter to send.

So here's to the fun, let's dream and explore,
Each twist and each turn, oh, who could want more?
In this humorous quest, our hearts have found home,
A journey realized, through laughter, we roam.

Fertile Grounds of the Unknown

In fields where weeds hold a parade,
The daisies cringe, they've been betrayed.
The tomatoes shout, 'We're ripe today!'
While carrots gossip in disarray.

A rabbit hops, wearing a crown,
Claiming the garden as his town.
While squirrels plan a nutty heist,
With acorns rolling, oh, how they spliced!

The sun's too bright, the worms too shy,
They wiggle and wriggle, asking why.
The pumpkins munch on leftover cake,
"Don't touch my frosting!" they all quake.

Oh, nature's dreams are quite absurd,
As flowers plot to spread the word!
Among the greens, pure chaos reigns,
In fertile grounds, laughter remains.

The Dichotomy of the Wild

In brambles thick and thickets deep,
Lies a raccoon that's lost in sleep.
With dreams of fish and pies so sweet,
But wakes to find a soggy seat!

A fox in heels struts down the lane,
While ducks quack songs of weather vain.
A bear recites old Shakespeare plays,
Yet forgets his lines, dances in rays.

The owls at night wear coffee cups,
And tell bad jokes while sipping up.
The deer roll eyes with knowing sighs,
As fireflies compete in firefly ties.

The wild is full of clumsy flair,
Where chaos reigns and none may care.
In every corner, laughter grows,
In bushes thick where humor flows.

Stitches of Nature's Tapestry

A fox with threads of gold and red,
Sews patches in a quilt for bed.
The mushrooms giggle, 'What a sight!'
As ladybugs join in, taking flight.

A stitch unravels, colors clash,
The rabbits jump in a panicked dash.
The butterfly pauses, quite bemused,
As nature's craft becomes confused.

Amidst the leaves, the hedgehogs whine,
"We need some order, it's design time!"
Yet nature chuckles, weaving on,
In every patch, where all belongs.

So let it be, this playful mess,
In stitches bright, we all confess.
Where laughter lingers, humorous reviews,
In nature's quilt of silly hues.

Beneath the Skyline of Ferns

Under ferns where secrets creep,
A snail does yoga, oh, so deep!
The ants perform a Broadway show,
While crickets chirp in 'Do-Si-Do'.

As shadows dance and mossy beds,
Explore delight where laughter spreads.
The owl grins, a spectral guide,
With jokes that leave the crowd tongue-tied.

A sloth hangs low, his thoughts resemble,
An artist's stroke, a slow disco tremble.
The frogs applaud in wild delight,
As breezes play with stars at night.

So come and laugh, beneath these ferns,
In nature's realm where humor churns.
For in this green, with joy we find,
The skyline's dance, both fierce and kind.

Journey Through Growth

In the garden, weeds do dance,
That carrot lost its second chance.
Tomatoes giggle in the vine,
While squirrels plot how to dine.

The sunbeams tickle leaves so bright,
As daisies wear their crowns of white.
A pumpkin's joke is much too tall,
Yet everyone will still enthrall.

The cucumbers play hide and seek,
While radishes whisper, 'Oh, so meek!'
Potatoes dream of being fries,
But they can't help but laugh and sigh.

So join this romp, the plants invite,
A sprout can find its day and night.
In soil's embrace, we'll giggle loud,
Together we are quite the crowd.

Foliage Fusion

Amid the leaves, a party brews,
Where mint and basil dance their blues.
Chard flirts with a sprightly pea,
While thyme keeps time with jubilee.

The tulips wear their silly hats,
And rabbits joke with coatless bats.
Beneath the branches, laughter flows,
As pollen tickles tiny toes.

An oak tree tells the best of tales,
About the days of windy gales.
While ferns do giggle, fanning out,
In all this laughter, there's no doubt.

As petals flutter, skies turn blue,
In this wild mix, life feels anew.
Every bud a punchline found,
In leaf-laden joy, we are all crowned.

Lush Reflections

In mirrored ponds, the frogs conspire,
To sing a tune that won't expire.
With lily pads as stage and flair,
Their croaks become a concert rare.

A dandelion blows a kiss,
To every passing breeze, pure bliss.
While willows sway, their arms so free,
Like dancers lost in jubilee.

The nature trails hold secrets bright,
Of fleeting joys and pure delight.
Chipmunks giggle at silly sights,
As daydreams spark through glowing nights.

In every shade, a riddle hides,
Each vine and sprout, their fate abides.
Reflect with laughter, let it bloom,
In nature's mirror, joy will loom.

Intersection of Souls

Under the arch of leafy way,
A squirrel spies on a bright buffet.
Here ants march on with steady beat,
While butterflies claim their wand'ring seat.

A hedgehog dreams of grand parades,
In acorn hats and leafy shades.
Crickets chirp their lullabies,
As nightingale winks, oh what a surprise!

The paths all twist and twirl around,
Where every footstep shares a sound.
From roots to crowns, all join as friends,
In this green world, joy never ends.

So laugh, dear wanderer, don't delay,
For in each bend, life plays its sway.
Together we find our heart's pure goal,
In the dance of nature, we meet our soul.

Elements of Nature

In a garden, a snail wore a hat,
Said, 'I'm off to see where the grass is at!'
The flower laughed, 'Oh please, you'll see,
You're slower than a gopher sipping tea!'

Birds chirped tunes, off-key and spry,
A squirrel danced with a piece of pie.
Bees buzzed around with a careless thrill,
While ants plotted heists on a downward hill.

The streams giggled, splashing with glee,
As rocks sat quietly, boasting with spree.
"I'm the best seat for the great fish's throne!"
They said with a wink, feeling right at home.

Then a breeze swooped in, tickling their sides,
The trees whispered laughter, swaying with pride.
Nature's own sitcom, a hilarious show,
Where even a worm can steal the spotlight's glow.

Chasing the Canopy

A monkey swung high in the canopy's depth,
Wearing sneakers, he seemed quite inept.
"Catch me if you can!" he called with delight,
But tripped on a liana, oh what a sight!

Down below, a raccoon, face black with mischief,
Planned to raid picnic baskets—that was his belief!
He donned a mask, thinking it chic,
But forgot the trail, oh so very weak.

The parrot squawked jokes, some old, some new,
"Knock knock," he said, "Who's there? Me and you!"
Foliage giggled, rustling the leaves,
While a lazy sloth dozed, dreaming of thieves.

At sunset, the chase turned to nap time,
Nature shared jokes, all in perfect rhyme.
Leaves sighed with laughter, branches did sway,
As night fell softly, in a humorous way.

Harmonious Trails

A frog sitting high played tunes on a reed,
Said, "Join my band, you're in for a deed!"
A turtle grinned wide, with his shell shining bright,
"Only if snacks are served, I'm quite the sight!"

The raccoons tap-danced on old, fallen logs,
While the skunks held their noses and giggled like frogs.
"Watch me leap," said one with a twitchy tail,
But slipped in the mud, sending trails up in hail!

While before them a path woven thick with delight,
Danced with the essence of day turning night.
"Don't fear the shadows!" the fireflies sang,
"Bloom where you're planted—and just let it hang!"

Harmony ruled with a funny old mix,
Where nature provided its own little tricks.
And every creature laughed under the moon,
For it's all pretty silly—just wait for the tune!

Green Echoes

A dandelion puff whispered a tale,
Of a brave little bug who decided to sail.
"I'm off to the breeze!" he declared with a cheer,
But forgot where he started—what a near sphere!

The wise old oak chuckled, shields of the sun,
"Remember your roots, before you get spun!"
While the daisies giggled, waving their heads,
Thinking of bugs by the tomatoes, in bed.

Then came the ants, marching in line,
Singing their anthem with a twist so divine.
"Move it, move it! We're late for our feast!"
And tripped on the daisies, oh! How they increased!

Echoes of laughter bounced off the leaves,
The whole forest whispered, "Can you believe?"
Nature held court in its funniest guise,
With critters and plants sharing laughs in the skies.

Unity in Bloom

In gardens where we all can tread,
Flowers mingle, a colorful spread.
Bees buzzing, dancing without a care,
Even the weeds find friendship there.

Together we laugh, together we grow,
Incessant chatter, a delightful show.
With vines and petals, we embrace our fate,
Bumbling like bugs, it's never too late.

Sprouting joy, alongside a gnome,
Who insists that he can knit at home.
Petunias gossip, daisies tease,
Life's just fun with a dash of breeze.

So here's to our patch, wild yet refined,
Where laughter and blooms are easily twined.
In unity's garden, we find our zest,
For in every petal, we are truly blessed.

Land of Flourishing

In this place where silliness thrives,
Every critter has a hundred lives.
Laughter grows on the trees overhead,
With jokes that are better than what's bred.

The carrots crack jokes about their size,
While the radishes roll their big round eyes.
Tomatoes blush when they hear a pun,
In this land, joy is never outdone.

A squirrel struts, claiming it's a king,
While the crows debate about fashion bling.
In this realm of knock-knock delights,
Every evening brings dazzling sights.

So revel, dear friends, in the sprightly air,
For here, the mundane has vanished—beware!
In sugar-sweet fields where we frolic and play,
Life's a banquet, and laughter's the tray.

Canopy of Dreams

Beneath the boughs, where giggles abound,
The acorns and squirrels share tales profound.
Sunlight will twinkle like winks from above,
As branches all sway with a rhythm of love.

A weasel in shades plays chess with a crow,
While the brook nearby takes a sparkling flow.
Wishes float down like leaves on the breeze,
With a chorus of frogs singing soft melodies.

The trees all gossip about who's the best,
As mushrooms hold court and put worries to rest.
With laughter like raindrops, the air's full of cheer,
Each moment, enchanted, brings friends ever near.

In this dreamland, absurdity's king,
With wonders unspoken, it's joy that we bring.
So come join the fun, there's a canopy wide,
Where play is the path, and adventure's our guide.

Infusion of Life

In a pot where flavors joyfully blend,
Spices do a jig, their own little trend.
Garlic and ginger tango and twirl,
As onions let out a squeaky swirl.

Bubbling broth sings a playful tune,
While veggies conspire to dance 'neath the moon.
Potatoes get cheeky, they take center stage,
In the stew of life, they're full of sage.

A pinch of humor with every dash,
Each meal occasion turns into a bash.
Whisking together all the fun we can find,
In a cauldron of laughs, we're whimsically blind.

So stir the pot well, let the flavors ignite,
With a splash of surprise, and a side of delight.
Life's an infusion, a fanciful blend,
With laughter as seasoning, let joy never end.

Fusion of Flora

In a garden where plants like to dance,
Petunias waltz in their flowery pants.
Daisies giggle, they can't keep still,
While roses blush with a sweetened thrill.

Lettuce chuckles at the sight they make,
As veggies join in, for goodness' sake!
The weeds laugh loudly, uninvited guests,
They think they're clever, but they're just pests.

A sunflower sways with a silly grin,
Telling knock-knock jokes as the day begins.
The herbs join in with a quirky rhyme,
In this playful patch, it's always prime.

Together they grow, a zany crew,
In vivid uniforms of every hue.
So if you wander to this funny scene,
You'll find laughter blooms in every green.

Intertwined Journeys

Two vines twist tightly with a playful tease,
Chatting on branches in the morning breeze.
One tells tales of a romp through the woods,
While the other describes their neighbor's goods.

A snail slides by, slow as can be,
Waving its shell, oh what a sight to see!
The flowers giggle, make all sorts of noise,
While ants, like children, enjoy their toys.

They plot a race, both stems bow and bend,
With mossy spectators, they cannot pretend.
A sudden gust sends them tumbling around,
And laughter erupts from the earthy ground.

In this green realm where quirks intertwine,
Silly stories flow like sweet vintage wine.
Every leaf nods, every stem kicks high,
Under a canvas of twinkling sky.

Corridor of Rebirth

In the land of sprouts, where the chuckles grow,
New shoots emerge like a rowdy show.
Every flower a comedian in repose,
With petals unfurling like jokes in prose.

A daffodil cracks a pun on the rise,
While daisies pretend to wear glasses and ties.
The soil beneath giggles, tickled by roots,
As laughter sprinkles like morning's glutes.

A old tree rolls its eyes at the noise,
Saying 'Why so loud? You're all just toys!'
But the lilacs assure him it's all in fun,
They flower in jest under the warm sun.

In this corridor where jesters reside,
Even the ferns feel a twinkling pride.
Laughter echoes, and joy takes flight,
A rebirth of humor beneath the sunlight.

Tranquil Convergence

Where streams chuckle softly and breezes sigh,
The flowers discuss who'll reach the sky.
Tall grass leans in with a curious ear,
Eavesdropping on petals spread far and near.

A bumblebee buzzes with a joke to share,
While ladybugs giggle with polka-dot flair.
The frogs croak songs, not always in tune,
Yet their melody's bright like a comic cartoon.

In this peaceful patch, mischief's afoot,
As clouds peek down, wondering what they put.
With whispers of humor amid all the green,
A tapestry woven, the funniest scene.

Despite the stillness, a riot unfolds,
With blooms that tell stories in petals of gold.
So if you wander to this tranquil place,
You'll find humor resting in nature's embrace.

Synthesis of Color

In a land where crayons fight,
Red says, 'I'm the one, take flight!'
Blue claims he can make it cooler,
While yellow laughs, 'I'm the ruler!'

Together they form quite a scene,
Sketching out all that can be seen.
A masterpiece in the purest glee,
Who knew colors could disagree?

Green pops up, quite out of place,
Says, 'I'm here to set the pace!'
But everyone just rolls their eyes,
As they blend in, to no surprise.

Like paint splatters all around,
Muddled shades never make a sound.
A funny mess of hues collide,
Turns out the joke's on color pride!

Vistas of Renewal

Once a hill that turned to mush,
Now a scene that gives a rush.
Nature laughed and grew some grass,
Cats lounged back, taking it en masse.

Birds now chirp with quirky tunes,
Finding nests beneath the moons.
But one brave snail took a stand,
Claimed his turf, 'This is my land!'

Dance like leaves in autumn's breeze,
Ticklish tickles make hearts freeze.
Fields of joy spread wide and far,
While grasshoppers drive tiny cars!

Turn the soil, plant some seeds,
Dust off the hat, fulfill your needs.
Laughter echoes through the trees,
New vistas sprout from silly pleas!

Oasis of Balance

In the desert, a sight to see,
Cacti play Monopoly.
'No hotels!' they shout and cheer,
Till tumbleweeds roll in with beer!

A pond where frogs croak lively tunes,
While sipping tea beneath the moons.
They discuss the art of leisure,
In this quirky, wobbly treasure.

Chameleons on every nook,
Reading books, oh, what a hook!
They change from green to vivid hues,
Debating what's the best to choose.

Balance found in nature's jest,
Life's a game, a welcome guest.
In this oasis, humor blooms,
Refreshing giggles fill the rooms!

Unearthed Connections

A worm once said with glee, 'Oh me!'
'I've traveled far, you'll just not believe!'
Underneath the soil, a grand parade,
Fiddling ants with tunes they made.

Roots gossip about the weather,
While petals ponder, 'Are we clever?'
Bumblebees buzzing in delight,
'We're the VIPs, popping in and out of sight!'

Digging deep, they form a chain,
Each little critter, none in vain.
Huddled close, sharing their tales,
In a world of laughter, no one fails.

So here's a toast to bonds that form,
In wacky places, outside the norm.
Unearthed connections, laugh and play,
Life's a rhyme without delay!

Mosaic of Renewal

In the park where colors meet,
All the squirrels dance to a beat.
They drop acorns, oh what a scene,
Nature's way of being mean!

Grass in stripes, oh what a sight,
Is it day, or is it night?
Flowers gossip, leaves confide,
In this patch where chaos hides!

Birds wear hats, a funny flair,
Singing tunes without a care.
While daisies try to keep it cool,
They can't help but break the rule!

Through laughter shared, our bonds renew,
In a world where whimsy grew.
Join the fun, let worries flee,
Amidst this wild, green jubilee!

Cascading Hues

A splash of color, what a show,
Roses giggle as they grow.
Tulips wink from their bright beds,
While dandelions shake their heads!

Leaves like hats on trees so tall,
Whisper secrets, hear them call.
Bright butterflies in line to glide,
Painting paths with every stride!

With each breeze, a jest they share,
While rabbits munch without a care.
In this frame of laughter's grace,
Anything can find its place!

So stroll along with cheerful cheer,
Join the nature's carnival here.
In a patchwork of pure delight,
Where humor reigns both day and night!

Verdant Embrace

In a forest where pine trees tease,
Laughter floats upon the breeze.
A chipmunk's prank, a funny feat,
Sneaks up quick to steal a treat!

Leaves converse, they sway and spin,
While bees hum songs, they can't win.
Nature's party, wild and free,
Join the fun, there's glee, you'll see!

Mossy carpets underfoot,
As frogs play hop, not one is mute.
Their croaks a tune, a silly croon,
In this green, we all commune!

So take a breath, embrace the scene,
Where every laugh's a joyful scream.
In this haven, ever bright,
We find our joy, our hearts in flight!

Passage of Time

Time ticks slow in grassy lanes,
Where squirrels are the ones with brains.
They bury nuts for winter's fun,
But forget where they're put, oh run!

Sunsets spill their colors wide,
While crickets play in rhythmic stride.
A turtle's race is never fast,
But cheers erupt as he moves past!

Clouds like sheep drift in the sky,
While frogs in lilypads ask why.
With every hop, they leap through time,
Spinning in a dance, sublime!

So let us laugh as hours fly,
In this garden, low and high.
Together, we will find our rhyme,
In nature's waltz, a joyful chime!

Emerald Pathways

In the park, the grass does dance,
Brought to life by ants in prance.
Joggers trip over secret routes,
Nature chuckles, oh how it shoots!

Bushes whisper, 'Who goes there?'
Squirrels play in wild dare.
With a hop and a skip, they tease,
While trees sway with the slightest breeze.

Veins of Nature

Look at that tree, it's got a grin,
Tickling leaves that feel like skin.
Rabbits argue, who's fluffiest here?
While owls hoot, 'You ate my beer!'

Flowers gossip in colors bright,
Bouncing laughter, pure delight.
Even bugs have parties at night,
As lanterns glow, they dance in flight.

Whispering Verdancy

Grass tickles toes, oh what a tease,
While bumblebees sing melodies with ease.
Frogs in the pond, dressed like a prince,
Croak out jokes, it's all in good sense!

Wandering vines, a maze quite absurd,
They've tangled up a lost little bird.
Chirping with glee, she finds her way,
Through giggling leaves that sway and play.

Threads of Hope

Laughter bounces from leaf to leaf,
A tapestry woven, joy's chief.
Clouds burst into giggles and cheer,
As sunlight winks, 'I'll stay right here!'

Raindrops slip on the smooth green blades,
Watering dreams, oh how it cascades.
And worms wiggle down with a sigh,
Saying, 'Oh dear, where's the pie?'

Echoes Through the Evergreen

In the forest, whispers play,
Squirrels chat in a nutty way.
Branches wave like arms in dance,
Even trees think they have a chance.

Mossy carpets soft and green,
Tumbleweeds that love to preen.
Nature's jokes, oh what a scene,
Life is goofy in between.

Boundaries in Blossom

Flowers giggle, petals bright,
Buzzing bees in pure delight.
A fence made of daisies, how grand,
Telling jokes that bloom on demand.

Butterflies in silly flings,
Chasing each other, flapping wings.
With every bloom, there's laughter free,
World's a stage in nature's spree.

Where Nature Paints Her Canvas

The painter spills her vibrant shades,
On trees that act like parades.
A canvas made of sunshine and cheer,
Color plans that logic can't steer.

Rivers giggle, tickling the shore,
While fish jump out, wanting more.
Nature's brush mixes work and play,
Life's an art show every day.

Hues of Hope and Harmony

In the meadow, laughter rings,
Birds compose their funny flings.
A rainbow bridged with giggling dew,
Even the clouds have jokes anew.

A whistling wind, a breezy jest,
Nature's comedy is the best.
Hope colored bright in every hue,
Life's a laugh, forever true.

Canopy Chronicles

In the trees, a squirrel prances,
Chasing dreams, and missing chances.
Leaves are laughing, branches sway,
Nature's fun, come join the play!

A bird with style, a silly dance,
Perched on high, it takes a stance.
Worms below are rolling eyes,
'Get a grip! You're bound to fly!'

Sunbeams waltz through leafy halls,
Casting shadows on the walls.
A rabbit hops with quite the flair,
Wishing it had not a care!

Life's a giggle, and a flip,
In this forest, friendship's hip.
Nutty tales from trees abound,
In this realm of laughs unbound.

Liminal Spaces

Between the worlds where shadows blend,
Funny things begin to bend.
A cat in socks, it takes a leap,
While ghosts just giggle, half asleep.

A door that creaks, a wall that sighs,
Whispers dance, like silly spies.
An umbrella that flies away,
'Guess it wants to join the play!'

A hat that thinks it's quite the star,
Waving at folks from near and far.
In this space, the odd is norm,
Where laughter's just a perfect storm.

Mind the gap, where jokes reside,
Along the edge, where ghosts confide.
Here, the quirky holds its place,
In this zany, silly space.

Earthly Whispers

The soil chuckles, roots interweave,
While daisies gossip, they believe.
A snail with swagger takes its trail,
It's zooming slow, a humor frail.

Rabbits twitch their ears so keen,
Eyes rolling at the grass so green.
Flowers prance in colors bright,
'Look at us, we're quite a sight!'

A frog in shades sings out its tune,
Croaking jokes from noon to moon.
The wind joins in, a playful breeze,
Tickling leaves, it aims to please.

Roots of laughter underground,
In this corner, joy is found.
Nature's stand-up, all around,
Whispers of humor, laughter's sound.

Nexus of Life

In a bustling hub where critters spree,
Life's a circus beneath the tree.
Bees in top hats, buzzing sweet,
Acrobats among the flowers' feet.

Ladybugs have tea to share,
Caterpillars hold a fashion fair.
Worms are digging up old jokes,
While ants form lines like silly folks.

Fireflies twinkle, lighting the night,
Drawing patterns, a dance of light.
Grasshoppers jump, with no delay,
'Life's a party, come out and play!'

In this nexus, wacky and wild,
Nature's funny, with every child.
Join the fun, don't miss the strife,
In this joyful web of life!

The Pathway of Flourishing Futures

In a field where daisies play,
Squirrels dance and fade away.
Chasing dreams in leafy lanes,
Bouncing high like playful trains.

With a twist and silly turn,
Frogs croak songs that make us yearn.
Past the trees that giggle low,
Oh, the fun we'll surely know!

Wandering Through Emerald Echoes

Through the woods we skip and hop,
Listening to the owls bop.
Mr. Bear wears silly hats,
And converses with his cats.

Every flower tells a joke,
Ticklish breezes make us poke.
Jumping streams, we splash about,
Giggles rise, there's never doubt!

Between the Veins of the Forest

In the shade where giggles sprout,
Wobbly deer spin all about.
Rabbits hide from snoozing birds,
All the while cracking absurd words.

Underneath the moon's soft gaze,
Frolicking in a playful maze.
With each tree a tale to tell,
We'll laugh and stumble, all is well!

The Division of Light and Leaf

When the sun splits the dancing shade,
Chickens argue, aren't they brayed?
On a lawn where laughter lingers,
Flowers wave with funny fingers.

Follow paths of wiggly greens,
Insects join our silly scenes.
Twirl and spin, oh what a hoot,
Nature's stage, a grand ol' fruit!

Earthbound Harmonies

In a meadow where daisies sway,
A squirrel steals snacks just for play.
Birds gossip about the best trees,
While rabbits hop in pairs with ease.

A frog tries to sing with no tune,
His croaks cause a nearby dog to swoon.
Butterflies dance with outrageous flair,
While ants march in lines, unaware of despair.

The sun's a dancer in a blue dress,
Yet some clouds come in, causing a mess.
A caterpillar thinks he's a star,
As he wiggles along, not going far.

Laughter floats in the summer air,
Nature's jesters, without a care.
In this vibrant and funny spree,
Life's upside down, so wild and free.

Experiments in Green

A scientist found a peculiar sprout,
It danced in the wind, causing a shout.
He took off his glasses to see it right,
But his hair got tangled in sheer delight.

With plants in lab coats, they plotted the deed,
To grow candy corn from a tiny seed.
But gumdrops bloomed on every tree,
And gummy bears shouted, "We're free!"

The beakers bubbled with minty cheer,
As grasshoppers bounced—you could hear them near.
"Oh, what a mix-up," the scientist sighed,
"Next time, I'll try to take it in stride!"

Yet laughter erupted as plants made a scene,
Chemicals laughing—oh, what a dream!
In this green lab where chaos is king,
They've confirmed that joy is a curious thing.

Pathways of Light

Two fireflies missed their glowing way,
Bickering loudly on a bright day.
One said, "Straight ahead! It's not hard!"
The other replied, "But I see a yard!"

They zigzagged across the buzzing bloom,
Avoiding a spider's glimmering gloom.
But oh, what a sight when they found the way,
A dance floor of stars to disco and sway.

The moon rolled over, chuckling so bright,
Watching two bugs in their silly plight.
They flashed like mad in a shimmering jig,
While critters around joined in, feeling big.

"Oh, pathways are funny!" the young bug did tease,
"Especially when we're lost in the leaves!"
With laughter and light, they zigged and they zagged,
In the glow of the night, their worries just lagged.

Scenic Restorations

A garden was tired, covered in weeds,
Until a raccoon came, full of bright ideas,
"I'll plant some balloons for a poppiest view,
And throw in some sparklers just for the crew!"

The daisies all laughed, with petals so wide,
While frogs clapped their hands and puffed out with pride.

"Is that a blue cupcake?" a robin then squawked,
As a gopher grew dizzy with all the talk.

The squirrels brought nuts, while the kittens brought cheer,
Turning drab into fab, month after month here.
A garden once boring was now quite the show,
With a rainbow of colors in everyone's glow.

"Let's throw a party!" bellowed the fox,
"Invite all the critters, let's take off our socks!"
With giggles and fun, they danced 'til the noon,
In a garden restored, where laughter was strewn.

Trailing Through the Leafy Veil

In a forest quite dense, where the ferns dance,
I tripped on a root, what a goofy chance!
The squirrels all giggled as I took a dive,
Said, "Join the party! You're quite the jive!"

The branches above formed a leafy parade,
While mushrooms below thought I was quite staid.
A raccoon then winked, said, "You've got flair!"
I laughed and replied, "I'm lost? Well, who cares!"

I thrashed through the trails with carefree delight,
Skipped over a puddle, and what a sight!
A frog in the mud gave a loud, hearty croak,
I grinned at him bright, said, "You're quite the bloke!"

But as gloom started rising, day turned to night,
I tripped on a log, oh what a fright!
Yet through all the chuckles and laughter I drew,
I found a way out—not too shabby, who knew?

A Journey Among Jade Shadows

In shadows of emerald, I strutted with glee,
Kicked up some dirt, what a sight to see!
A snail saw me coming, said, "Take it slow!"
I winked and said, "Buddy, you should join the show!"

A leaf dropped like candy from the sky so bright,
I snatched it in air, oh what a sweet flight!
But then there was tea, brewed with rain and sun,
Charmed critters showed up, oh, this day's fun!

With a laugh and a jig, we danced on the greens,
To the tune of the bugs and the rustling scenes.
From the tall grass came whispers, jokes flying the best,
As my momma would say, "Just forget all the rest!"

In the end, I found treasures in laughter and cheer,
Among all the jesters, I wasn't a mere.
As the sun set behind, life felt so complete,
In this party of green, how could I retreat?

The Splintered Route of Growth

I stumbled through thickets, what a silly sight,
Branches fought back, gave my head quite a fright.
The flowers were laughing—yes, I swear it's true,
Chided me gently, "You're late! Who knew?"

The trees were all gossiping, branches a-flutter,
Said, "Here comes a clutz, let's watch him mutter!"
I fell in a puddle, splash! Went the game,
The frogs led a cheer, shouted, "Join our fame!"

With a wink and a grin, I climbed a nearby stump,
A ladybug giggled, while I went to jump.
"Do it again!" yelled a squirrel with a glee,
You'd think I was dancing on top of a tree!

But through splintered pathways, my path still remained,
A wacky adventure where nobody feigned.
With the friends I had made, I wouldn't trade a thing,
In the end, I just laughed through the joy life can bring!

Beneath the Canopy of Change

Under a ceiling of leaves, I fumbled about,
With acorns and twigs as my new scout route.
A chipmunk was peekin', said, "What's your plan?"
I shrugged with a grin, said, "I'm no grand man!"

Through canopies dripping with sunlight and fun,
Every tree sang a tune, inviting to run.
But then came a splash from the nearby pond,
A plump duck started quacking, how could I respond?

"Come dance with me, sweetie, let's whirl 'round the bend,"
Fell in quite the puddle—who knew ducks could blend?
The whispers of leaves turned to chuckles galore,
Be it this crazy route, I couldn't want more!

So here I shall wander, through laughter and cheer,
With the quirky of nature, there's nothing to fear.
In this world of mischief, where jokes rarely change,
Life's an adventure beneath this fun canopy range!

The Hidden Trail of Renewal

In a forest where squirrels play,
Each branch swings in a silly ballet.
Trees giggle with leaves in a dance,
While mushrooms plot their next prank by chance.

Raccoons wear masks, so dapper, I swear,
As they scheme under everyone's stare.
Beneath the ferns, trouble brews,
In this comedy where nature takes cues.

Pinecones drop like clumsy old bombs,
Warning us not to disturb their psalms.
With each step, laughter bounces around,
As I trip over roots with a foolish sound.

Nature's giggles echo through space,
Every bush hides a cheeky face.
So let us roam without worry or care,
In this hidden trail, fun hangs in the air.

Walking a Lush Divide

On a path where daisies gossip and bend,
I strut with a confidence hard to defend.
Butterflies dazzling in riotous hue,
Flap by like they own this avenue.

A frog croaks a joke, oh what a thrill,
While a snail competes in an epic hill.
Each step's a chuckle, with every glance,
Nature throws humor into the dance.

The sun winks down, a silly little star,
Casting shadows that play, suggesting ajar.
A bird squawks loudly with comic flair,
As I trip on the grass, splat without care.

With laughter erupting from branches above,
Every creature seems to spread some love.
In this lush divide, where smiles collide,
Joy is the treasure that we can't hide.

Memories in a Grove of Dreams

In a grove where whispers tickle the leaves,
Old oaks chuckle at the fun they perceive.
The wind seems to tease with a light airy flirt,
As I dodge acorns, protecting my shirt.

Underneath branches where shadows conspire,
A rabbit juggles, a skilled little liar.
With each bounce, he throws off my aim,
As I stumble, he's winning this playful game.

Fireflies join like a sparkly parade,
While I recount every blunder I've made.
Nature's a storyteller, weaving the night,
With laughs wrapped in moonbeams, pure delight.

In this dreamlike grove, where mishaps prevail,
Each fond memory brings a hearty exhale.
Among the branches, joy floats in beams,
Creating laughter in a world of dreams.

Shades of Serenity and Strife

In a landscape where calm meets a wild spree,
Llamas wear sunglasses, oh so carefree.
They laugh off the troubles that echo and flow,
While I tumble through hedges, in riotous show.

The brook babbles nonsense, a true jokester,
As frogs wear their crowns, plotting to foster,
A kingdom of quirks, filled to the brim,
With adventures that dance on a whimsical whim.

Even the daisies seem to have jokes,
Giggling softly as I dodge pokes.
A spider spins tales with a silky finesse,
Each thread holds a giggle, never a mess.

Through shades of joy, where laughter takes flight,
Every mistake feels endlessly bright.
In this blend of peace, where humor thrives,
We find shades that paint our joyful lives.

Blooming Crossroads

At the junction where daisies dance,
A bee took a chance on a flower's romance.
But they laughed and they buzzed, in a comedy show,
While weeds rolled their eyes, 'What a silly tableau!'

In the shadows of shrubs, a squirrel steals sight,
With acorns aplenty, he thinks he's quite bright.
But slips on a leaf, oh what a surprise!
As nature giggles, it's hard not to sigh.

Labyrinth of Greenery

In a forest of laughter, paths twist and twine,
A rabbit called Fred thinks he'll carve out a shrine.
But he lost his way, hopped in circles like mad,
As birds in the trees cawed, 'Oh Fred, you're so rad!'

With a wiggle and jiggle, he sidesteps and spins,
While mushrooms enliven the dance of his sins.
But the trees just chuckle, as Fred trips again,
Life in this maze is a whimsical zen!

Living Boundaries

Oh, hedges that whisper and fences that squeak,
Count the squirrels in line that they magically sneak.
But who needs a border when the chickens unite?
With more clucking and strutting, oh what a sight!

A tortoise named Timmy is bound to take lead,
While the rabbits all giggle, 'Slowpoke, pick up speed!'
Yet Tim grins and chuckles, 'I'll finish this race,
I'm teaching you all a slow-motion embrace!'

Pathways of Serenity

On a path paved with petals, a llama trots through,
Wearing shades like a star, his coolness in view.
He stops by the pond, strikes a pose in reflection,
While ducks quack in tune, like a comical section.

A troll under bridges tells jokes made of mud,
To creatures who chuckle and wiggle with crud.
'Just take life with flair!' he sings with a grin,
'For laughter's the treasure in every thick skin!'

Enchanted Trail

In the woods, a path does twist,
Where squirrels dance and fungi exist.
A lost shoe lies under a tree,
Perhaps it belongs to a gnome, you'll see!

Trees wear hats made from old tin cans,
While ants march out in conga lines, their plans.
Barking dogs join the silly parade,
Spin and twirl, in sunlight, they wade.

Berries burst in vibrant hues,
A feast of nature, a berry cruise.
Look out! A deer with a borrowed tie,
Trying its best to look quite spry!

So lace your boots and join the fun,
On this happy trail under the sun.
Each turn will spark a giggle or two,
Adventure awaits! Come, join the zoo!

Bounty of the Earth

A pumpkin grew with a cheeky grin,
Claiming the title of veggie kingpin.
Carrots in sunglasses, veggies unite,
Having a rave under the moonlight!

In the garden, a tomato sings,
In hopes of finding summer flings.
'Look at me, I'm red and round!
Why is that beet just underground?'

Cabbages gossip about the corn,
Saying, 'Who's the fairest since we were born?'
The radishes snicker in playful jest,
As they watch peas having a contest!

So harvest joy from this earthy spree,
Where laughter and friendship grow like a tree.
Bring a basket and fill it with cheer,
Nature's bounty is waiting right here!

Haven of Harmony

In a tiny nook where breezes flow,
A rabbit wears socks, in case it can't sew.
Hummingbirds show off their ballet skills,
While bugs play chess on the garden's hills.

The raccoons host a tea party grand,
With acorns and berries, it's simply unplanned!
A soft raccoon serves cupcakes with a grin,
While owls play melodies on violins!

In this haven of laughter and glee,
Squirrels and chipmunks form a jubilee.
With marshmallow clouds above the scene,
Nature's orchestra feels like a dream!

So come take a seat on the grass so green,
Join in the fun, sweet like whipped cream.
With a wink and a smile, you're part of the crew,
In this joyful place, where fun is all new!

Borders of Life

A fence where daisies tickle their toes,
Chickens play tag, as laughter glows.
A cow plays hide-and-seek just for fun,
Saying, 'You'll never see me, I'm number one!'

While bees in sunglasses zoom to and fro,
Planning to party beneath the sun's glow.
Frogs at the pond host a karaoke night,
Singing sweet songs, oh what a sight!

Cats chase the shadows, thinking they're fast,
But the shadows are clever, they're never harassed.
With each little giggle, a story unfolds,
In a world where humor never grows old!

So wander along these edges of cheer,
Where borders are blurred, and fun is near.
Every corner a burst of delight,
In this land where smiles take flight!

A Hueman Canvas

In a park so bright and wide,
Picnic baskets take a ride.
Squirrels plotting, oh so sly,
Stealing crumbs, they're quite the spies.

Joggers tripping on their lace,
Chasing ducks, a silly race.
Who knew grass could be so slick?
One wrong step and that's the trick!

Children giggle, mud-streaked legs,
Painting joy as nature begs.
Splashes here and splashes there,
Laughter floats upon the air.

A canvas green, a silly spree,
Nature's art, wild and free.
Underneath this sky so blue,
Every step's a laugh anew!

Verdant Odyssey

A path so lush, where whispers reign,
Wandering feet dodge puddles' gain.
An ant parade in single file,
Drawing laughs with style and guile.

Frogs croak tunes, a ribbit band,
With polka-dot jumps on every land.
The wind might tease with ticklish breeze,
While trees sway gently with playful ease.

Picnics set with ants as guests,
While sandwiches play at being the best.
Giggling mushrooms, cheeky fawns,
Surprise us all at the break of dawn.

Each twist and turn a comic plot,
Nature's humor hits the spot.
In this place where laughter sings,
Adventure's path is crowned with springs!

Secrets of the Thicket

In tangled brush where shadows creep,
A dandelion tries not to weep.
Its fluffing head, all blown around,
Makes wishes dance, then tumble down.

A hedgehog waddles, quills on snooze,
In search of berries, dodging shoes.
Birds tell tales of silly fights,
While butterflies share dizzy flights.

With every rustle, laughter pours,
As woodland critters play theirScores.
The secrets held in leafy lairs
Enchanting hearts with funny snares.

Sticks and stones may break some bones,
But mossy beds are cushy zones.
In this thicket, fun prevails,
As giggles echo through the trails!

Whispers of a Verdant Path

On a winding road of emerald kiss,
Where sunbeams play and shadows twist.
A snail retreats with a fancy shell,
Its slow parade casts a funny spell.

Butterflies wear their finest suits,
While flowers dance with goofy roots.
Dancing leaves join in the spree,
Nature's joy, wild and free.

A gopher peeks from his earthy home,
Squirting dirt in a silly comb.
Critters laugh at his muddy try,
While birds just chirp and sigh, oh my!

The whispers here, a vibrant cheer,
In every step, you'll feel sincere.
Join the fun on this green ride,
Where nature's charm is bona fide!

www.ingramcontent.com/pod-product-compliance
Lightning Source LLC
Chambersburg PA
CBHW071852160426
43209CB00003B/521